Nature > Nurture

Taylor Heywood

BookLeaf Publishing

Presentation by *BookLeaf Publishing*

Web: www.bookleafpub.com

E-mail: info@bookleafpub.com

ISBN: 9789357616102

First edition 2022

I would like to thank Nephenee, Cheyenne, Vlaski, Ray, San and Iain. I couldn't do it without you.

ACKNOWLEDGEMENT

I acknowledge the land I live on belongs to the Haudenosaunee, Anishinnabeg and Attawandaron peoples. I'd like to make this acknowledgement because this book is all about my relationship to the natural world around me, and it wouldn't be right to release this book without honouring the traditional and rightful owners of this land, who worked tirelessly to protect the environment that now touches my heart enough to want to write about. Every day I am learning more about the ongoing genocide against Indigenous people, things that just weren't taught in school. I will do my best to contribute to righting these wrongs, and I hope that when we look towards nature for comfort and peace, we do not forget about the work we still must do to correct the pain this country is inflicting towards Indigenous people.

This land should be returned to it's rightful keepers, nature should be treated as sacred again, and the genocide against Indigenous people must be ended for good.

PREFACE

To be enjoyed one poem a day, or all at once, I just hope you enjoy it.

in, out

Skin stretched miles wide.
History on display like
a girl with nothing to hide.
Green, a blanket for a tired world.
The pines grow so close together.

Crows are on the road.
My hand is on your leg.
We drive through remnants of explosions,
in awe of the cuts we overcome.

Breathe.
Just breathe.

A tiny joy to fill your lungs.

hush

Sing to me, wombed in fields and lakes.
Feel me kick, habits I leave as little gifts.
With a gentle hand I make history face itself.
Embraced by the lakes on the left, greeted by the
gravel on the right.
I am hugged, I am held.
Precious north,
comfort me,
comfort me.

little village

I saw the stars for the first time,
walking with a lantern by Agawa Bay,
my attention split a million ways.
How many ships followed the prettiest star and
fell off the earth?
Pine air fills my mending lungs, green and black
make a palette in the sky.
The chuckling birds make light of the dark.
Tiny squirrels plan heists for a meal.
Come little village, rest in my hands as long as
you need before you dance with the leaves.
I watch growth in slow motion, Saplings holding
hands with the mushroom beneath my feet.
Simple as time itself, just close your eyes and
count the wind.
3AM and the highway roars, I thank this place
for all it's joy,
drifting off on my mattress pad laying on the
grey tent floor.

weathered

Cupped hands at the neck of the creek, watering
the garden in my gut. I dance in the sliver of
moonlight, a shadowbox girl with her feet dug
into the soil.

My atoms learned the words just not the choreo.
I spin and spin, so fast I can't see the crowd - but
they see me, sandy skinned, with stories tattooed
on my tongue, almost ready to become.

mirror

I opened up my heart to the quiet,
the ringing in my ears an unwelcome parade.
I march at the beat of my own drum and look
crazy to the silenced.
I stand in a field like a scarecrow,
I lay in the fountain like loose change.

Is this what it feels like to be seen?
To be really seen; not just passed and forgotten
like deadlines.
I am half here,
my eyes hollow to the gaze of pity.
See in me what you see in yourself.
Mirrored girl, speak your mind.
Release the storm in your head,
seek the truth in the pines and grow a backbone.
Treat yourself holy,
hope like heaven for sturdy ground.
Fight like hell for the confidence they ripped
from your shaking hands.
Hold still, child of the moons pull.
Grass is growing from the soil in your gut.

saved

Thin as the air or myself in 06,
Self assured on the top of Whistler.
Saw valleys as vast as belief
in dragons and fairies and various beasts.
Sanity knocks but I'm not at the door,
there's a knot in my stomach that keeps me
ashore.

My soul is a lighthouse and I was a ship,
barrelling t'wards a familiar abyss.
Sat in my mind had a picnic with it,
laughed over crackers and cried quite a bit.

Wild what willpower will overcome.
Finding your might is a fight that for some
is too much to bear, but oh not I.
If the map doesn't save you, look to the sky.

roots

I found my heart on Sommers Road jumping off
the pile of clothes and playing Mario Kart 64.
I soaked in the moments like a dirty sponge,
clear of mind but filthy from the mud around the
campground.
I felt a hurricane pass, prayed for peace to a god
I soon abandoned while holding a hand that
would soon grow cold.
I watched myself become a sinkhole, dragging
everyone around me down when I thought I was
inviting them in.
I raised myself when nobody else could, I took
control of the powerlessness.
I visit my hometown like an archaeologist.
I find places I remember like I was taught them.

The air is still mint.
The people still stop when I cross the street.
But

I am distant,
I am a wave that returns and leaves again.
I am building up strength,
and smoothing stones.
I will make myself whole, again.

rosewood

Gardenkeeper,
tell me is it wise to spend the night?
I pruned the stems so carefully
but the roses have still died.
tell me is that natural or have I messed things
up?
I'll stay all night and try again if I'll have better
luck.

Woman,
Staying longer won't fix what's come and past.
I know you tried so carefully,
Some things aren't meant to last.
Tell me why the roses mean so much?
Is this a hobby or a crutch?

Gardenkeeper,
Maybe I'll put it another way.
I must create this time,
instead of ruining what I've made.

Woman,
Every maker has to settle with defeat.
I see a bud, right there beside your feet.
Be kind, tomorrow give it another try.
The birds thank you, and so do I.

gentle hypocrite

I write of nature while on my bed,
surrounded by trinkets and other useless things.
I'm nesting but there's nothing I hold sacred.
My feet are easy scapegoats.
They burn like sinners in the sun.
They ache like hearts pumped by others so long
they stop beating on their own.
Still, It's too easy to make excuses.
Too easy to procrastinate until it's late.

The woods are too close
for the distance I have built.
I'm slowly taking steps
but I'm burdened by the guilt.
Comforting myself is a challenge I face because
I heal at the wrong time and the wrong place.
But that's all I can ask as a girl by myself.
A tongue made of acid, a shit bill of health.

Maybe I'll go for a walk after this
and sit by the stormwater management pit.

at bay

Waves from the bay bring out the child in me.
Smiling pictures at Mahoney's Beach.
Baseball cap on the top of the stairs.
A kid unaware of how brief they'll be there.
Life was Yahtzee at the trailer yard and
making new rules for Pokemon cards.
I remember it differently now,
hiding when my brothers took it too far.

My mother killed herself.
Drowned in the Ocean that gave me strength.
I'm a tree and my roots are tangled.

We drove for two days, a place called Guelph.
I searched for worth in everyone else.
My mind continued to block it out.
I lived the next few years in a cloud.

The pain made me hide away.
I latched onto vices to keep the nightmares at
bay.

Now I'm clean, I cut the rope.
Hold onto me like I hold onto hope.

cover

I watched the teeth sink in from behind the
glass.
170 km wind gusts through my home.
Waited on baited breath for the next text.
"I'll be OK. Always," my sister says.

I saw the street wash away on Twitter.
I watched the downtown crumble to it's knees
while I take a piss.
Then I turned off the app.
Got distracted.
Spent another hour watching prison dramas.

Everyone' safe,
the ones I know.
I'm 3 floors up as my province sinks below.

I can tune it out, and pretend it's gone.
Like trailer roofs, and business awnings.

unabandon

Write about nature, this isn't about me.
It's not supposed to be another soapbox
for me to play the victim like it makes a
difference.

Sunlight on a nice day.
Moss wet from fresh dew.
A tree growing on a rock.
Loving myself as much as I loved you.

Things I've seen, things I've tried.
I lost the plot, I'm stuck inside.

Tomorrow, tomorrow I'll take that walk.
Visit the frogs at the swamp.

that walk

Pineapple express and a strawberry fill.
No glasses so the trail blurs.
The clouds circle like there's blood in the water.
"This path closed July to December"

Time to detour around the Wholesale Club.
This is the third parking lot I've seen that
Manulife owns..
Time to walk past the rich men with their private
lake,
and past the ornamental apples that squish to the
touch.

Back to my bench, covered in moss.
Seven ducks in the seaweed swamp.
Took a couple jackets but I made it out.

Tiny chirps and the rustling of leaves.
Chainsaws at the closed path.

Is this the closest taste on my tongue?
A manmade hole half a block from the mall?
I give thanks for surviving with me.
Finding life among the concrete.
Am I just here to write a book?
Does my soul still yearn for creature comfor-

coexist

I got interrupted by a squirrel,
looked me in the eyes and yelled in fear.
It ran away when I got too close.
I hope to prove I belong here.

brilliance

A seabound girl on a cliff by the lake,
who convinced herself it's the Atlantic.
She drove through the blasted rock
and thanked the glaciers for something mighty to
ponder.
I can't survive outside the face of brilliance.
A flat field is a flat line.
I know, I know, I'm full of myself.
I'll give you faith, just give me time.

gossip

The air cools from the winds on the lake.
The berries shrivel and cover the ground.
Slow motion how the prospects collide.
A deck of cards falling one at the time.
Summer turned it's face on us.
Reasoning older than you.
Trees lose their passengers.
A hidden bench enters view.
This time of year makes intentions known.
I intend to sit with tea and gossip with the
evergreens.

i

Queen of self erasure, view and viewer split like
wood.
"i" scribbled and erased, scribbled and erased til
the pencil breaks.
For years the pages have seen my heart dripped
onto them, a coffee pot beating.
Now returns the urge to erase myself,
to continue a legacy that once appalled me.
Maybe my poetry would be better if it was
written by a ghost,
observing but not affecting, devoid of spirit or
stakes.
Maybe it's best if my thoughts never rest,
a pressure cooked repressed.

There's trees in my family tree.
Ambition has somewhere to be.

clay shape

I'm not the girl I was before.
I am clay shaped hardened tryna soften my
edges.
I look death in the eye, blue like mine, blue like
lakes I want to die in.
Or wanted, it's hard to remember to use the past
tense.
Even harder to believe it.
I lost parts of me I can't get back.
I lost hope that was carried by the breeze.
I fund strength I didn't know I had
and god damn it I wish I still didn't.
I wish things were different.
I wish my mind wasn't a god damn motel.
I see pain as an old friend.
I see resistance as mundane,
some days more than others.
I've gone through hair colours like lovers.
I change myself with the moon.
Or I change myself like the tide,
back and forth, back and forth until the jagged
rocks turn to sand.
I've never understood the point of ignorance.
I know too much - it's own battle.
Maybe life is made for a girl with a small heart.

One day I hope that changes
but I won't be the one to change it.
I'm just a girl with an umbrella in a hurricane.
I'm just looking for a bus shelter that isn't
shattered to pieces.
I'm just looking.

where would you like to reserve?

I spend my days helping people go to parks,
sitting at a desk destroying my back.
I count the minutes til my next break,
while my head aches and my knuckles crack.
I created a life where I eat sleep and work,
paying off my debt but there's nothing left.
I sat in stasis for 8 years, paralyzed by the fear
of rebirth.
Fresh air, I'm almost there.
I overdose on care.
I need 3 more nights of sleeping in, a blunt to
myself and a good fuck.
I need a hand to hold and a four leaf clover for
good luck.
I bought a park pass I'll use this week,
Go to Sauble Falls or Craigleith.
I'll buy my permit online,
and spare those working instead of me.

horizon

Rise, hunter moon.
We stand in awe of your dandelion flesh.
Shine down on the fish swimming up the falls.
Memorable be the taste of an uphill battle.
I shiver in the sweetest way.
Under the moon, I am just another reflection,
just another wind swept thing.

the right day

The line between self love and self hate is
dotted.
I switch lanes quicker than personalities.
I like using fancy words, acting like my brain is
an altar, not altered.
I set goals then kick them back, clawing closer
to an ending I'm rewriting as we speak.
I'd be 2 inches taller if my back was straight...
would be a little bit richer if I was too.
I'm a Leo, I can't sit on the sidelines.
No popcorn for me thanks - I'll be on screen.
I'm in the muck, searching around the edges of
my heart for any moments to exploit.
I'm too hard on myself, this is Exhibit A.
I'm trying to learn, trying to grow, trying to
teach.
And yet, here I am again, prey to my own
tendencies.
I'll break this habit like my mothers back after
all the cracks.
Honestly,
I love myself.
On the right day.
Under the cricket hum, I hold my own hand in
the evening sun.